D1243315

SUPER SPORTS STAR

RANDY MOSS

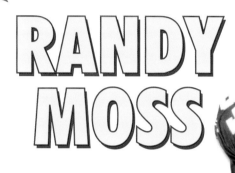

Stew Thornley

Enslow Publishers, Inc.

40 Industrial Road   PO Box 38
Box 398   Aldershot
Berkeley Heights, NJ 07922 Hants GU12 6BP
USA   UK

http://www.enslow.com

Library of Congress Cataloging-in-Publication Data

Thornley, Stew.
    Super sports star Randy Moss / Stew Thornley.
        v. cm. — (Super sports star)
    Includes bibliographical references and index.
    Contents: High hopes — A star in the making — Getting another chance— Leading
the Herd — Rookie sensation — Pouring it on.
    ISBN-10: 0-7660-2049-5
    1. Moss, Randy—Juvenile literature. 2. Football players—United States—
Biography—Juvenile literature. [1. Moss, Randy. 2. Football players. 3. African
Americans—Biography.] I. Title. II. Series.
    GV939.M67 T49   2003
    796.332'092—dc21   2002004248

ISBN-13: 978-0-7660-2049-8

Printed in the United States of America

10 9 8 7 6 5 4 3 2

To Our Readers: We have done our best to make sure all Internet Addresses in this book
were active and appropriate when we went to press. However, the author and the pub-
lisher have no control over and assume no liability for the material available on those
Internet sites or on other Web sites they may link to. Any comments or suggestions can
be sent by e-mail to comments@enslow.com or to the address on the back cover.

Photo Credits: © Mark Brettingen/NFL Photos, pp. 6, 8, 40; © David Drapkin/
NFL Photos, p. 34; © Allen Kee/NFL Photos, pp. 4, 10; © Al Messerschmidt/NFL
Photos, p. 1; © Steven Murphy/NFL Photos, pp. 13, 18; © Vincent Muzik/NFL
Photos, pp. 11, 16, 22; © Joe Patronite/NFL Photos, p. 38; © Al Pereira/NFL Photos,
p. 24; © J.C. Ridley/NFL Photos, pp. 27, 32; © Joe Robbins/NFL Photos, pp. 29, 31;
© Todd Rosenberg/NFL Photos, p. 36; © David Stluka/NFL Photos, p. 44; © Tony
Tomsic/NFL Photos, p. 20.

Cover Photo: © Associated Press.

CONTENTS

Introduction

A wide receiver is one of the most exciting players in football. Receivers catch passes—often long passes. Receivers are the big-play people. Catching a long pass and scoring a touchdown can turn a game around.

A receiver has to be able to get open and catch the ball. There are a few qualities that make a good receiver: Some are fast, others have great moves, and many of them are good jumpers. Most importantly, most receivers are great at catching the ball.

Very few receivers have all these talents. One who does is Randy Moss. Moss is a great player for the Minnesota Vikings. He does not catch as many passes as some receivers. But the passes he does catch are for big gains or touchdowns. Sometimes Moss catches a long pass. He can also catch a short pass and then run a long way with it.

Moss is tall. He is six feet, four inches. He has great leaping skills. Add that to his speed, and it is easy to see why he is so hard to defend.

Randy Moss jumps
over a defender.

Players who try to cover Moss know how tough he is to stop. Donnie Abraham is a defensive back for the Tampa Bay Buccaneers. He says sometimes it looks like Moss is not running hard. But Abraham is not fooled. Moss can turn on the burners and blow right by a defender. Moss can also change directions when he is at full speed. "He doesn't have to do a lot of shaking to get by you," says Abraham.

Moss knows how good he is. He says, "My moves help me get past defenders and get to where I'm going: the end zone."

High Hopes

CHAPTER

The Minnesota Vikings were ready for a great year. It was the first game of the 1998 season. The Vikings had a high-powered offense with great receivers. Two of them, Cris Carter and Jake Reed, had proven themselves in the NFL. The Vikings had another receiver they had big hopes for. This one—Randy Moss—would be playing his first game.

Moss had been the first player picked by the Vikings in the NFL draft a few months before. The NFL draft is the way that professional football teams pick new players each year. Now the Vikings would see if they had made a good choice.

It did not take long to find out. On the third play of the game, Moss caught an 11-yard pass from Brad Johnson. A few minutes later, he caught an even bigger pass.

The pass came late in the first quarter. Moss took off as the ball was snapped. As he got downfield, he looked back. Johnson was throwing a pass to him. But the pass was not

Randy Moss was the first player the Minnesota Vikings picked during the 1998 NFL draft.

long enough so Moss slowed down. Floyd Young, who was covering Moss, also put on the brakes. The two leaped and fought for the ball. Moss tipped the ball in the air, and Young reached for it but missed. Moss reached out and grabbed it. It was a great play. It was good for a 48-yard touchdown.

Before the half was finished, Moss had another big catch. This time he burned Donnie Abraham, the Tampa Bay Buccaneers' best cornerback. Shaking free of Abraham, Moss caught a pass for a 31-yard touchdown.

Receivers have to be able to catch the ball and run for the touchdown.

The Vikings beat the Buccaneers, 31–7. Moss had four catches totaling ninety-five yards and two touchdowns.

"I know I'm not ready for everything that comes with the game in the NFL," said Moss after the game. "But I think I came up big today. I just wanted to make things happen today and show people that I can play on this level against any team."

Donnie Abraham said of his opponent that day, "He's not the greatest receiver we've ever faced, but he's going to be."

★★★ UP CLOSE

Since 1998, Randy Moss has 44 TDs in 48 games. He has even thrown a touchdown pass.

CHAPTER 2

A Star in the Making

Randy Moss was born on February 13, 1977, and grew up in West Virginia. He has a sister and a brother. All were raised by their mother, Maxine Moss. Randy's father was a man named Randy Pratt. But Moss had little contact with his dad.

Moss's mother worked hard to teach her children right from wrong. The family lived in the small town of Rand, not far from Charleston, the capital of West Virginia.

Moss was good in sports when he was a kid. He played baseball, basketball, and football and ran track. He was very fast. His speed paid off in all these sports.

Moss went to high school in the nearby town of Belle. He was a sports star at DuPont High School. In baseball, he played center field.

He was so good that professional scouts came to watch him play.

He was even better in basketball. His leaping ability came in handy. Moss's coach, Jim Fout, said, "He does things you've never seen anyone else do." Moss was twice named the high school basketball player of the year in West Virginia. One of Moss's friends was Jason Williams. The two played together on the DuPont High School basketball team. Williams now plays basketball in the National Basketball Association (NBA).

In track, Moss won the state championship in the 100-meter and 200-meter dash.

However, Moss may have been at his best in football. He could do it all. On offense, he was a great receiver. On defense, he was a safety. A safety is a defensive back who covers receivers. Moss did well at safety. Of course, he never had to cover a receiver as good as he was.

Moss also returned punts and kickoffs. He also did the team's punting and place kicking.

Randy Moss played many
sports when he was a kid.

A team could not ask for more from a player. With Moss, the DuPont Panthers won two state championships. Moss was named the football player of the year for West Virginia his last year of high school, or senior, season.

By this time, Moss was thinking about where he would play football next. As he grew up, he watched a lot of college football. The team he enjoyed watching the most was Notre Dame. Notre Dame is a college in Indiana with a great football program. Moss watched players like Tim Brown and Raghib "Rocket" Ismail play for Notre Dame. They were great receivers. Brown even won the Heisman Trophy, which is awarded each year to the best player in college football.

Moss knew he was a great receiver. He dreamed about playing for Notre Dame.

Moss would have that chance. But he would also lose it.

CHAPTER 3

Getting Another Chance

Randy Moss was a young man with a lot of special skills and talents. But he was not perfect. Like anyone else, Moss made mistakes. Some were bad mistakes that almost cost him his future.

Moss learned from his mistakes. He learned because they hurt him a lot.

In 1995, Moss was offered a scholarship to go to Notre Dame. That meant he would play football there, and the college would pay for his education and books. However, Moss got in trouble his last year in high school. He was involved in a bad fight. For his part in the fight, he had to go to jail. Sleeping in a jail cell made him think about what he had done. "I pretended it was just a place to sleep," he said.

"I'd get up the next morning and do what I had to do. It just humbled me."

Because of the trouble he got in, Moss lost his freedom. But he lost more than that. Notre Dame took back its scholarship offer. Moss went to Florida State University. Coach Bobby Bowden did not let him play football his first year. He wanted Moss to adjust to college life first. Moss was redshirted. That meant he had to sit out a season. "That was fine with me," said Moss. "I had so much to learn."

Even though he did not play in the games, Moss attracted attention. He ran the 40-yard dash in 4.25 seconds. That is very fast. Bowden had

Randy Moss had to sit out a season at Florida State.

only one player who had ever run it faster. That player was Deion Sanders, who became a star in the NFL. Sanders also played major-league baseball.

Moss looked like he would be a star, first in college and then in the NFL. He looked forward to being able to play for Florida State in 1996. But then he got into more trouble. He smoked marijuana and got caught. Bowden dropped Moss from the team and he lost his scholarship to Florida State.

Moss's mistakes had now cost him a chance at two different colleges. He wondered if he would get another chance. If he did, he wanted to make the most of it. Moss came back to his home state and enrolled at Marshall University in Huntington, West Virginia. Marshall was a smaller school. The bigger schools like Notre Dame and Florida State competed in football at the Division I-A level, the top level. The Marshall Thundering Herd played at the

Division I-AA level. They hoped to move up to the higher level.

The Thundering Herd of Marshall was a power in Division I-AA. They had won the national championship in 1992. In 1995, they made it to the Division I-AA championship game but lost to the Montana Grizzlies. Their new coach, Bob Pruett, hoped the Thundering Herd could make it one step further. Pruett had

By his second season at Marshall, Moss was thought of as one of the best receivers in college football.

played for Marshall in the 1960s. He wore number 88. That is the number Randy Moss wore when he came to Marshall.

Some people thought Pruett was taking a chance with Moss. What if he got in trouble again? But Pruett stood by his player. "I knew Randy beyond what people knew about him from headlines," he said. "I believe strongly that he deserved this chance."

Marshall's first game was against Howard University, which had a good team. Moss had a great game. He caught three passes for 134 yards, including a 76-yard touchdown. He also returned five kickoffs for more than 140 yards. On top of that, Moss landed a key block on a long touchdown run by Erik Thomas.

It was a good start for Moss. It would get even better.

CHAPTER 4

Leading the Herd

Moss was a business major at Marshall. But he showed that football would be his career.

Marshall beat Howard, 55–27, in the 1996 season opener. The Thundering Herd kept rolling. Moss led the team. Marshall won all eleven of its games in the regular season. Moss had nineteen touchdown catches in those games.

He added nine more in the playoffs. Four of those were in the championship game. The Herd played Montana for the title. Moss scored the first touchdown in each of the four quarters. He grabbed a 19-yard pass for a touchdown in the first quarter. That put the Herd in front, 7–0. Early in the second quarter, Moss caught a long pass from Eric Kresser.

It was good for a 70-yard touchdown. Kresser and Moss hooked up for a 54-yard touchdown in the third quarter. Moss caught a 28-yard pass for a touchdown in the fourth quarter. Led by Moss, the Thundering Herd beat Montana, 49–29. They were the champions of Division I-AA college football.

Counting the playoffs, Moss had twenty-eight touchdown catches for the season. That tied a Division I-AA record. The record was held by Jerry Rice—the greatest receiver in the history of football. Moss was in good company.

So was the Thundering Herd. They were too good for Division I-AA. They moved up to the top level, Division I-A, of college football in 1997. Marshall faced better competition. To Moss, it did not matter. He was still awesome.

Some defensive backs enjoyed the chance to play against Moss. It helped them learn how good they were. One said, "You look at somebody who is going to be drafted in the first round, and then you look at yourself. Now I see

In 1997, Randy Moss won the Fred Biletnikoff Award. This award is given to college football's top receiver.

where I have to get to reach where I want to go. It's like a self-challenge that allows me to see what I can do against players that good."

Moss had ninety-six catches in 1997 for more than 1,800 yards. Those are huge totals. He won the Fred Biletnikoff Award as the best receiver in the country. He also finished fourth in the voting for the Heisman Trophy.

Marshall won ten games and lost two during the regular season. That earned them a spot in the Motor City Bowl in Pontiac, Michigan. Marshall played the Mississippi Rebels. The Herd fell behind, 7–0. But Moss helped them tie it with an 80-yard touchdown catch. It was a wild game that Marshall finally lost, 34–31.

It was also the last college game for Moss. He could have played two more years for Marshall. But he already knew the game at that level.

Randy Moss was ready for the NFL.

Rookie Sensation

Moss was the best receiver in the NFL draft in 1998. Everyone knew how good a player he was. "Our scouts say he's the best receiver to come out of college in the last 30 years," said Dave Wannstedt, coach of the Chicago Bears.

However, some teams were bothered by some of the past trouble Moss had been in. Because of that, many teams passed up the chance to draft him. One team was happy to see that happen. The Minnesota Vikings wanted Moss. But a lot of teams drafted before the Vikings. All those teams selected someone else. When it was the Vikings' turn, Moss was still available.

That is how Moss became a Minnesota Viking. The Vikings already had a good team. With Moss, they figured they would have a great team. "Randy is a big, smooth athlete," said Vikings head coach Dennis Green. "There are very few receivers who have his big-play capability after the catch. He brings tremendous down-the-field speed."

Minnesota planned to break Moss in slowly. After all, they already had some good receivers. Moss could take his time and learn from them. But Moss came up big in his first game. His two touchdowns against the Tampa Bay Buccaneers showed the Vikings they could not hold him back for long.

By the third game, Moss was a regular in the lineup. At Green Bay in early October, Moss had two long touchdowns. Overall, he had five catches for 190 yards in the game. In doing

Randy Moss races downfield.

so, he led the Vikings to their fifth win without a loss.

Moss liked playing in the Metrodome in Minnesota. The stadium has a big screen at each end. The screens show action from the game as it happens. Moss used that to help him. As he started downfield, he would glance up at the big screen. Without turning his head, he could see if the pass was coming his way. "I've learned to look at the screen while playing," he explained. "I do it a lot. It's not a gift or a talent. It's just how fast your eyes are. It's all in your head. If you can run and look at the screen, it's somewhat to your advantage."

As a rookie, Randy Moss set and broke many team records.

Moss used the big screen to help him the next time the Vikings played the Green Bay Packers. The Vikings were clinging to a six-point lead. It was midway through the fourth quarter. Minnesota had the ball at the Green Bay 49-yard line. It was third down, and they had nine yards to go. They could try a shorter pass to pick up the first down. Or they could throw the bomb and go for it all.

Having a player like Moss made the decision easier. The Vikings went for the big play. Moss took off and looked at the screen. He saw the pass thrown his way. "Then I had to leave the screen alone and look up for the ball," he said. By this time, Moss was running down the sideline. Packers cornerback Rod Smith was right with him. The pass was underthrown. Moss cut inside Smith and caught the ball at the 10-yard line. He stayed on his feet and made it into the end zone. It was another great touchdown. By this time, Vikings fans were getting used to these kinds of plays from Moss.

Randy Moss leaps for the ball as a defender tries to stop him.

The Vikings finished the regular season with fifteen wins and one loss. It was the best record in the NFL. They won their first playoff game. Their next game was against the Atlanta Falcons. It was for the National Football Conference (NFC) championship and a spot in the Super Bowl.

Minnesota was favored to win. However, Atlanta pulled off a shocker. The Falcons won the game in overtime, 30–27.

It was a tough way to end the season. But it had still been a great year for the Vikings. Moss was a big reason Minnesota did so well. No one with the Vikings was sorry the team had picked Moss in the draft.

Moss gave credit to Dennis Green for taking a chance on him. "Coach Green took a lot of heat for this," said Moss, "but he just caught a steal. They brought me here to play football and score touchdowns and put points on the board. That's what I'm focusing on, and hopefully I'll fulfill all my dreams."

CHAPTER 6

Pouring It On

oss had done it all his first season. He tied a Vikings record with seventeen touchdown catches. That was also an NFL record for first-year players, or rookies. He was named the NFL's Rookie of the Year.

Was it luck, or was he really that good?

In 1999, Moss answered the question. He was that good. He had eighty catches during the season. His catches covered 1,413 yards. That was the highest total in the NFC. It was also a Vikings record.

He also returned one punt for a touchdown. He even threw a touchdown pass. He took a handoff and looked like he was going to run with the ball. Instead he fired to Cris Carter for a 27-yard touchdown. Moss became the first Vikings receiver ever to throw for a touchdown.

Minnesota did not repeat its 1998 success. The Vikings had a 10–6 record in the regular season. They made the playoffs, but they were knocked out before the NFC championship game.

Randy Moss was named the Pro Bowl's Most Outstanding Player in 1999.

Moss had another great year, though. He went to the Pro Bowl, the NFL all-star game. Moss led the NFC to a 51–31 win over the American Football Conference (AFC). Moss set a Pro Bowl record with nine catches and 212 receiving yards. He was named the Pro Bowl's Most Outstanding Player.

In 2000, the Vikings got off to a fast start. The team won its first seven games. Minnesota slowed up in the second half of the year. They still won the championship in the NFC Central Division. Moss had a lot of big games during the season. On Thanksgiving, the Vikings played at Dallas. Moss had 168 receiving yards and scored three touchdowns.

He came up even bigger in the Vikings first playoff game, even though he caught only two passes. However, he turned them into two terrific plays. The game was scoreless in the first quarter. Moss caught a short pass near the sideline. He then got past two tacklers and turned it into a 53-yard touchdown. In the

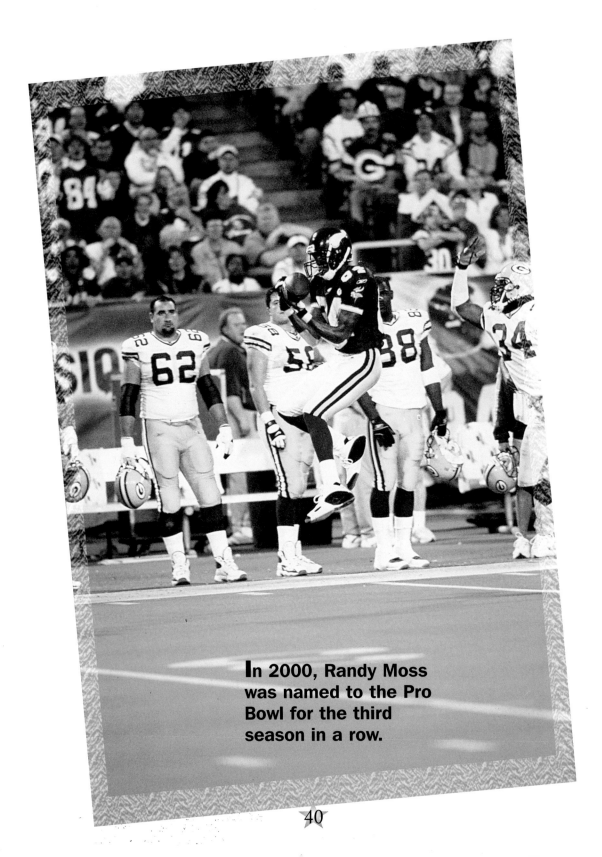

In 2000, Randy Moss was named to the Pro Bowl for the third season in a row.

second half, he took an even shorter pass and turned it into an even longer gain. This one was good for a 68-yard touchdown. Minnesota beat New Orleans, 34–16.

Then the Vikings faced the New York Giants for the NFC championship. But they lost again, only a step away from the Super Bowl.

Moss is young and will have many more chances to make it to the Super Bowl. He has a lot going on besides football. He is involved in the community. In Minnesota, Moss has a program called Randy's Purple Pioneers. It is a charity program at a children's hospital.

Moss has two children of his own. He has a daughter, Sydney, and a son, Thaddeus.

During the off-season, Moss plays basketball. Sometimes he plays for fun. But other times it is more serious. In the summer of 2001, Moss played for the Pennsylvania ValleyDawgs of the United States Basketball League.

Moss plays basketball to stay in shape. He also fishes and swims to have fun and relax.

But most of his attention is still on football. He wants to be the best in the game. Some think he already is.

Mike Sherman, coach of the Green Bay Packers, says, "Moss is the scariest man in football and the best player, talentwise. You hold your breath every time they snap the ball."

On March 2, 2005, Moss was traded from Minnesota to the Oakland Raiders. He was traded to the New England Patriots on April 29, 2007, where Moss will play his best for his new team.

★★★ UP CLOSE

Randy Moss was named 2000 Pro Bowl Most Outstanding Player after setting records for catches and receiving yards.

CAREER STATISTICS

NFL						
Receiving						
Year	Team	GP	Rec.	Yds.	Avg.	TDs
1998	Minnesota	16	69	1,313	19.0	17
1999	Minnesota	16	80	1,413	17.7	11
2000	Minnesota	16	77	1,437	18.7	15
2001	Minnesota	16	82	1,233	15.0	10
2002	Minnesota	16	106	1,347	12.7	7
2003	Minnesota	16	111	1,632	14.7	17
2004	Minnesota	13	49	767	15.7	13
2005	Oakland	16	60	1,005	16.8	8
2006	Oakland	13	42	553	13.2	3
Totals		**138**	**676**	**10,700**	**15.8**	**101**

Rushing						
Year	Team	GP	Att.	Yds.	Avg.	TDs
1998	Minnesota	16	1	4	4.0	0
1999	Minnesota	16	4	43	10.7	0
2000	Minnesota	16	3	5	1.7	0
2001	Minnesota	16	3	38	12.7	0
2002	Minnesota	16	6	51	8.5	0
2003	Minnesota	16	6	18	3.0	0
2004	Minnesota	13	0	0	NA	0
2005	Oakland	16	0	0	NA	0
2006	Oakland	13	0	0	0	0
Totals		**138**	**23**	**159**	**6.9**	**0**

GP—Games Played   **Att.**—Rushing Attempts   **Avg.**—Average Yards per Catch/Run
Rec.—Receptions   **Yds.**—Yards Receiving/Rushing   **TDs**—Touchdown

Where to Write to Randy Moss:

Mr. Randy Moss
c/o New England Patriots
One Patriot Place
Foxborough, MA 02035

According to Randy Moss, his biggest sports thrill is, "Catching a touchdown pass and hearing the crowd go wild."

WORDS TO KNOW

blitz—A play where the defense rushes with more than its linemen. Linebackers and defensive backs may rush the quarterback on the blitz.

cornerback—A defensive back. It is his job to cover receivers.

draft—A selection of players by teams, who take turns choosing the players they want.

freshman—A ninth-grade student in high school or a first-year student in college.

fullback—The fullback is normally called upon whenever short yardage is needed. He is usually the most powerful runner on the team. He can drive straight ahead into the line or block for other runners.

Heisman Trophy—The award that is given each year to the best college football player in America.

junior—An eleventh-grade student in high school or a third-year student in college.

line of scrimmage—The place that the play starts on the field.

nose guard—A defensive player who usually lines up over center.

quarterback—He is in charge of the offense. He calls the plays, sometimes with help from the bench. The quarterback can either pass the ball, hand it off to a running back, or keep it and run.

redshirt—A college player who does not play for his college team for a particular year. He will not lose a year of eligibility.

rookie—A player in his first full season in professional sports.

sack—To tackle a quarterback attempting to pass the ball behind the line of scrimmage.

safety—Another defensive back who covers receivers, like a cornerback. A safety is also a play when the defense tackles a player in his own end zone. The defensive team gets two points if it gets a safety.

scholarship—An award that allows a player to attend college for free.

scout—A person who watches players and determines how good they are.

secondary—If a runner gets past the line of scrimmage, he has to get past the players in the secondary further downfield.

senior—A twelfth-grade student in high school or a fourth-year student in college.

sophomore—A tenth-grade student in high school or a second-year student in college.

Super Bowl—The NFL's championship game.

tight end—Usually a big player who catches passes and blocks for runners.

veteran—A player with many years of experience.

READING ABOUT

Bernstein, Ross. *Randy Moss, Star Wide Receiver.* Berkeley Heights, N.J.: Enslow Publishers, Inc., 2002.

Minnesota Vikings Staff. *Minnesota Vikings.* Ed., CWC Sports, Inc. White Plains, N.Y.: Everett Sports Publishing & Marketing, 1998.

Stewart, Mark Alan. *Randy Moss: First in Flight.* Brookfield, Conn.: Millbrook Press, Inc., 2000.

Internet Addresses

The Official Site of the Patriots
<http://www.patriots.com>

Randy Moss
<http://www.nfl.com/players/12576_bios.htm>

INDEX